Selection of patients with stable angina for further inv

David R Murdoch
Specialist Registrar in
Henry J Dargie
Professor and consulta
MRC Clinical Research Initiative in Heart Failure
University of Glasgow
Glasgow G12 8QQ

Introduction

Angina pectoris is a common condition that affects approximately 1% of the United Kingdom population aged between 30 and 59 years, and 2.6% of those aged over 60 years. It is a clinical diagnosis, usually characterised by a combination of chest, throat or arm discomfort which is precipitated by exertion or emotion, and relieved by rest. Discomfort may also be felt in the jaw, gums, temples, back or epigastrium. Sometimes the patient experiences breathlessness rather than discomfort and this, or a variety of other symptoms, may be referred to as an 'angina equivalent'. While many patients with mild or moderate symptoms are diagnosed in the community, only a minority of patients with angina are currently referred by their general practitioner (GP) for a specialist opinion[1].

Why investigate patients with stable angina?

The investigation of patients with stable angina may be undertaken to:

1. Confirm the diagnosis;

2. Estimate prognosis; *and*

3. Identify those who may benefit from intervention.

As the severity of symptoms bears an inconsistent relation to the severity of disease[2], most patients with typical symptoms of angina should be routinely referred for prognostic assessment. Patients with very extensive coronary disease, such as left main-stem stenosis and severe triple-vessel disease, have a greater chance of survival following bypass surgery than with medical treatment alone[3]. Intervention for prognostic improvement currently entails coronary artery bypass surgery as, while angioplasty can be useful for symptom control, there is no evidence that it prolongs survival[4].

Whom should we investigate ?

Table 1 refers. Most patients with typical symptoms should be considered for investigation, but the urgency of referral depends upon the severity of the symptoms. Where there has been a sudden change in the frequency or severity of anginal episodes, or pain occurs at rest, patients are considered to have unstable angina and, in most cases, should be admitted to hospital as an emergency. Such patients have a much higher risk of death and acute myocardial infarction than those with stable angina, and this risk can be substantially reduced by anti-thrombotic therapy with heparin and aspirin.

Patients with recent-onset exercise-related angina, particularly those who fail to respond quickly to standard anti-anginal therapy, also constitute a high-risk group. With a rate of fatal myocardial infarction or death in the year following a new diagnosis of around 4%, and of non-fatal myocardial infarction of 7%, prompt referral for outpatient investigation is desirable.

For other patients with more prolonged symptoms of stable angina, priority for investigation should be given to those who are likely to gain the most from intervention - ie, those with the most severe symptoms - and other evidence of increased risk (especially left ventricular dysfunction) as suggested by a prior history of myocardial infarction or heart failure.

Table 1: *Selection of patients with stable angina for further investigation*

Urgency of referral	Patient group
Immediate/urgent	Rest pain
	Sudden increase in severity or frequency of angina
	Recent onset angina not responding to treatment*
Early	Other recent onset typical angina*
	Stable but severe symptoms
	Angina with prior myocardial infarction or heart failure
Routine	Prognostic assessment in most patients with well controlled symptoms (subject to other factors such as concurrent illness or advanced age)
	Atypical non-limiting symptoms

* Patients with recent onset angina should receive appropriate treatment on diagnosis; treatment should not be witheld before further investigation.

Whom should we not investigate ?

Investigation, on prognostic grounds, is probably inappropriate in elderly patients (perhaps in those aged over 75 years), and for those with a clear diagnosis but in whom severe concomitant disease would make surgical intervention unreasonable. In addition, a few patients will decline referral, having had a full discussion of the risks and benefits of investigation and the possibility of surgery explained.

Which test for which patient ?

Preliminary examination and investigation: Clinical examination in patients with angina is often unrewarding, but is a prerequisite to exercise testing. It is necessary to look for possible precipitating causes such as aortic stenosis, anaemia or thyrotoxicosis. A standard resting 12-lead electrocardiogram (ECG) is often normal even in the presence of extensive coronary artery disease[5]. However, an ECG which is abnormal in any way supports the clinical diagnosis of coronary artery disease and identifies a population with a poorer prognosis[6]. Serum cholesterol and haemoglobin should be routinely measured and thyroid function tests performed where there is clinical suspicion of an abnormality.

Exercise tolerance testing remains the most useful investigation in the diagnosis and prognostic assessment of angina and is increasingly available via GP open access facilities. If the recognised contra-indications are observed, most notably unstable angina and significant aortic stenosis, it is a safe and well-tolerated procedure with an incidence of only 0.3 to 1.9 serious complications per 10,000 tests. ST segment depression during exercise is the hallmark of myocardial ischaemia but, while it does not occur in all patients with coronary artery disease, it develops in some patients with a normal coronary arterial tree. The exercise test is reliable in a population with a high prevalence of coronary disease, although when the prevalence is low (eg, in young women with atypical symptoms) the frequency of false-positive results becomes unacceptably high. The appearance of ventricular tachyarrhythmias or a significant fall in systolic blood pressure during exercise also identifies patients at a high risk of future acute myocardial events, irrespective of ECG changes.

An exercise tolerance test (ETT) provides an objective assessment of the severity of symptoms and of the degree of functional limitation, it is often useful even when left bundle-branch block or left ventricular hypertrophy complicate accurate ST segment analysis. Exercise time is a useful measure but is highly dependent upon the chosen exercise protocol. The conversion of workload achieved to metabolic equivalents (METS) allows more standardised comparisons of functional capacity to be made. Prognostic assessment based on symptoms, the extent of ST

4

segment deviation, and workload achieved selects those patients who should go forward for coronary angiography[7]. The diagnostic and prognostic information from exercise testing is not significantly compromised while patients are taking anti-anginal treatment and, since abrupt discontinuation of beta-blocker therapy is associated with a significant risk of precipitating unstable angina or acute myocardial infarction, it is our policy not to discontinue anti-anginal therapy before exercise testing.

Radionuclide myocardial perfusion imaging is a useful alternative to exercise tolerance testing for those who are unable to exercise because of immobility, peripheral vascular disease or obstructive airways disease. It is also valuable where the presence of resting ECG abnormalities, such as left bundle-branch block or left ventricular hypertrophy, preclude exercise ECG ST segment analysis. If the result of an ETT is equivocal, myocardial perfusion imaging is a useful adjunct, especially for women in whom false-positive ETTs are common. A variety of pharmacological stress agents such as dipyridamole, adenosine or dobutamine can be used. These are usually combined with limited exercise, most often on an exercise bicycle, to decrease uptake of the isotope by the gut and to improve image quality. Currently thallium (^{201}Tl) is the preferred isotope, but technetium (^{99m}Tc) is gaining popularity due to reduced radiation exposure and improved image quality. In experienced hands, myocardial perfusion imaging can provide diagnostic and prognostic information similar to that provided by the exercise ECG. However, it is expensive, involves radiation exposure, and image quality can be attenuated by breast shadows in women.

Stress echocardiography: Examination of the heart by echocardiography during pharmacological or exercise stress is gaining popularity for the assessment of myocardial ischaemia, especially in patients with suspected left ventricular dysfunction. It has the advantages of avoiding radiation exposure and of giving an accurate assessment of ischaemia, left ventricular function and valvular abnormalities at a single examination. The test relies on the principle that progressive stress will induce myocardial ischaemia and reduce contractile function in the area of affected myocardium. When there is reversible left ventricular dysfunction (myocardial hibernation), affected myocardium shows a characteristic biphasic response to stimulation, whereby contractile function improves at low levels of inotropic stimulation but subsequently deteriorates at high level stimulation. This can predict which patients may experience improvement in left ventricular function following revascularisation by percutaneous transluminal coronary angioplasty (PTCA) or coronary artery bypass grafting (CABG). As the identification of new wall motion abnormalities is highly dependent on image quality, the technique is less suitable for patients with obstructive airways disease or marked obesity.

Other tests: Ambulatory ECG monitoring is sometimes used to identify episodes of myocardial ischaemia that are not accompanied by typical angina pectoris (silent ischaemia). However, it is now becoming clear that the presence of silent ischaemia in stable angina pectoris during ambulatory monitoring gives no more information than that obtained from the exercise ECG[8].

What about left ventricular function ?
In the context of angina, the presence or absence of left ventricular dysfunction is the single most important prognostic factor. The Coronary Artery Surgery Study (CASS) showed that the prognosis for patients with single-vessel disease, but significantly impaired left ventricular function was worse than for those with triple-vessel disease in whom left ventricular function, was preserved[9]. Furthermore, those with left ventricular dysfunction have a proportionately greater survival advantage from surgical revascularisation[10]. If the resting ECG is normal, significant left ventricular dysfunction is unlikely to be present[11]. In patients with an abnormal resting ECG, the investigation of angina should include an objective measure of left ventricular function such as echocardiography.

What about women ?

Women with chest pain are treated differently from men[12]. They are more likely to experience atypical symptoms because of the higher prevalence among women of less common causes of ischaemia, such as vasospastic and microvascular angina, and syndromes of non-ischaemic chest pain such as mitral valve prolapse. In addition, women have a lower prevalence of angiographically-proven coronary disease, even in the presence of typical symptoms[13]. Significant coronary artery disease remains unusual in pre-menopausal women, and following the menopause women lag approximately ten years behind their male counterparts in their prevalence of symptomatic myocardial ischaemia, except among patients with diabetes mellitus where any female advantage is eliminated.

Unfortunately, the investigation of chest pain in women is more difficult than in men. Exercise tolerance testing is complicated by a high prevalence of exercise-induced 'ischaemic' ECG changes in healthy asymptomatic women. Therefore, the result of the ETT should be interpreted along with an assessment of the pre-test likelihood of disease based on age, hormonal status, and the presence of cardiovascular risk-factors. While a normal test remains reassuring, those with an equivocal test or those with an apparently 'ischaemic' test in whom the pre-test likelihood of disease is considered to be low often require additional investigative procedures such as radionuclide myocardial perfusion imaging or coronary angiography.

As mortality from ischaemic heart disease remains the leading cause of death in women in the UK, it is important that clinicians are aware of possible bias and ensure that gender does not unduly influence referral or investigation patterns.

Who should have coronary angiography ?

Criteria for referral: Patients with stable angina who have mild non-limiting symptoms and a good exercise tolerance on treadmill testing are likely to have a favourable prognosis and do not routinely require invasive investigation[14]. However, those with severe symptoms despite adequate medical treatment, with angina occurring early (probably within a month) after acute myocardial infarction or in whom the severity of ischaemia (assessed by non-invasive testing) would suggest the presence of severe coronary disease should be referred for coronary angiography.

Limitations: Coronary angiography gives a unique detailed anatomical record of the coronary arteries and their stenoses. However, strictly speaking, it does not diagnose myocardial ischaemia since it does not give full physiological information about the effect of stenoses on myocardial perfusion. Nevertheless, it is an essential prelude to intervention and provides valuable information for risk stratification.

Conclusions

- Coronary artery surgery improves survival for patients with severe coronary artery disease - ie, left main-stem stenosis or triple-vessel disease with impaired left ventricular function.
- The severity of symptoms of angina may not reflect the severity of the underlying coronary artery disease.
- An abnormal resting ECG identifies a group of patients with a less favourable prognosis, many of whom will also have impaired left ventricular function.
- For most other patients with stable angina, assessment by exercise tolerance testing will aid selection of high-risk patients who should proceed to coronary angiography.
- Pharmacological stress tests can be used for those patients unable to perform an exercise test. Radionuclide scans are useful when exercise testing gives equivocal results or for patients in whom exercise testing is inappropriate.

References

1. Clarke KW, Gray D, Hampton JR. Implication of prescriptions for nitrates: 7 year follow-up of patients treated for angina in general-practice. *Br Heart J* 1994; **71**: 38-40.

2. Hultgren HN, Peduzzi P. Relation of severity of symptoms to prognosis in stable angina pectoris. *Am J Cardiol* 1984; **54:** 988-93.

3. European Coronary Surgery Study Group. Long-term results of prospective randomised study of coronary artery bypass surgery in stable angina pectoris. *Lancet* 1982; **2:** 1173-80.

4. RITA-2 trial participants. Coronary angioplasty versus medical therapy for angina: the second randomised intervention treatment of angina (RITA-2) trial. *Lancet* 1997; **350:** 461-8.

5. Norell M, Lythall D, Coghlan G, et al. Limited value of the resting electrocardiogram in assessing patients with recent onset chest pain: lessons from a chest pain clinic. *Br Heart J* 1992; **67:** 53-6.

6. Miranda CP, Lehmann KG, Froelicher VF. Correlation between resting ST segment depression, exercise testing, coronary angiography, and long-term prognosis. *Am Heart J* 1991; **122:** 1617-28.

7. Mark DB, Shaw L, Harrell FE Jr, et al. Prognostic value of a treadmill exercise score in outpatients with suspected coronary artery disease. *N Engl J Med* 1991; **325:** 849-53.

8. Dargie HJ, Ford I, Fox KM. Total ischaemic burden European trial (TIBET). Effects of ischaemia and treatment with atenolol, nifedipine SR and their combination on outcome in patients with chronic stable angina. *Eur Heart J* 1996; **17:** 104-12.

9. Emond M, Mock MB, Davis KB, et al. Long-term survival of medically treated patients in the coronary artery surgery study (CASS) registry. *Circulation* 1994; **90:** 2645-57.

10. Alderman EL, Fisher LD, Litwin P, et al. Results of coronary artery surgery in patients with poor left ventricular function (CASS). *Circulation* 1983; **68:** 785-95.

11. Davie AP, Francis CM, Love MP, et al. Value of the electrocardiogram in identifying heart failure due to left ventricular systolic dysfunction. *BMJ* 1996; **312:** 222.

12. Steingart RM, Packer M, Hamm P, et al. Sex differences in the management of coronary artery disease. *New Engl J Med* 1991; **325:** 226-30.

13. Weiner DA, Ryan TJ, McCabe CH, et al. Exercise stress testing. Correlations among history of angina, ST-segment response and prevalence of coronary artery disease in the coronary artery surgery study (CASS). *New Engl J Med* 1979; **301:** 230-5.

14. Gordon DJ, Ekelund LG, Karon JM, et al. Predictive value of the exercise tolerance test for mortality in North American men: the lipid research clinics mortality follow-up study. *Circulation* 1986; **74:** 252-61.

Antivenoms and treatment of snake-bite

David A Warrell
Professor of Tropical Medicine and Infectious Diseases
Centre for Tropical Medicine, University of Oxford
John Radcliffe Hospital
Oxford OX3 9DU

Introduction

More than 100 people bitten by Britain's only indigenous venomous snake, the adder (*Vipera berus*), are treated in hospital each year. Although severe envenoming is not rare, only 12 people have died of adder bite this century, the last being in 1975. Increasing numbers of exotic venomous snakes are kept, legally and illegally, and these cause at least five notified bites annually. The two important groups are *Viperidae* (vipers, adders, pit vipers, rattlesnakes) and *Elapidae* (cobras, kraits, mambas, coral snakes and Australasian snakes).

Biological effects of snake venoms

Snake venoms contain 20 or more components, mostly proteins, which include:

- enzymes such as the procoagulant serine proteases and arginine esterhydrolases that activate the blood clotting cascade leading to disseminated intravascular coagulation;
- proteases responsible for tissue damage;
- phospholipases A_2 that damage membranes and block neuromuscular transmission;
- zinc metalloproteinase haemorrhagins that cause spontaneous systemic bleeding by damaging vascular endothelium; *and*

- non-enzymatic polypeptide toxins such as the post-synaptic neurotoxins that bind competitively with acetylcholine.

Other components of pharmacological interest include bradykinin-potentiating compounds, angiotensin-converting enzyme inhibitors and sarafotoxins, highly homologous with endothelins.

Clinical features in the bitten person

More than one-third of those bitten by venomous snakes develop no signs of envenoming.

Adder (Vipera berus) bites

Local pain and swelling usually develop within minutes. Swelling, lymphangitis and bruising may advance rapidly to involve the whole limb within 24 hours. Systemic symptoms may appear within five minutes of the bite - eg, vomiting, abdominal colic, diarrhoea, shock, angio-oedema, urticaria, and bronchospasm. Hypotension may be transient, persistent, recurrent or progressive and may be fatal. Electrocardiogram (ECG) abnormalities are common and include ST or T wave changes, heart block, arrhythmias and evidence of myocardial infarction. Severe anaemia may develop. Coagulopathy and spontaneous bleeding into the lungs, gut or urinary tract are uncommon, while acute renal failure, adult respiratory distress syndrome (ARDS) and cerebral oedema are rare complications.

Bites by exotic snakes

While local swelling is usually detectable within two hours of envenoming by vipers, bites by some elapids may cause no local signs. Tender enlargement of regional lymph nodes draining the bitten area is an early sign of envenoming. Bleeding from the gums indicates a haemorrhagic diathesis (vipers, Australasian snakes) whereas bleeding from venepuncture sites and wounds suggests coagulopathy. Hypotension and shock result from hypovolaemia, vasodilatation or cardiotoxicity (vipers). Anaphylactic reactions may occur. Ptosis is the earliest sign of neurotoxic envenoming in patients bitten by elapids and a few species of vipers. Trismus, generalised muscle tenderness and stiffness with passage of black/brown urine suggest rhabdomyolysis.

Laboratory investigations

In patients bitten by venomous snakes, blood should be taken on admission for full blood count, routine biochemistry and tests of blood coagulation, and urine tested for blood/haemoglobin/myoglobin and protein and by microscopy to detect haematuria and red cell casts. In patients bitten by exotic vipers and Australasian elapids, blood clotting tests should be repeated six-hourly until they return to normal after antivenom treatment. The peripheral neutrophil count is raised. Initial haemoconcentration, resulting from extravasation of plasma, is followed by anaemia caused by bleeding or, more rarely, haemolysis (exotic vipers). Thrombocytopenia, prolongation of clotting times and elevation of fibrinogen degradation products occur after bites by vipers and Australasian snakes. Serum creatine kinase and aspartate and alanine aminotransferase concentrations are raised after severe local envenoming and generalised rhabdomyolysis. Table 1 lists investigations in cases of adder (*Vipera berus*) bites.

Treatment of snake-bite

First aid

The victim should be transferred to the nearest General Practitioner (GP) surgery or hospital as quickly and comfortably as possible, avoiding

Table 1: *Checklist of laboratory investigations in cases of adder (Vipera berus) bite*

1.	Full blood count
2.	Clotting studies
3.	Creatinine, enzymes (creatine kinase, aminotransferases)
4.	Urine microscopy and urinalysis
5.	Electrocardiogram, chest x-ray

active movements especially of the affected limb. The bitten limb should be immobilised, as far as is practicable, with a splint or sling. Traditional first aid methods are potentially harmful and should not be used - these include local incisions, suction, instillation of potassium permanganate, and tourniquets. Bites by neurotoxic elapid snakes may cause respiratory paralysis within a few hours and 'pressure immobilisation', which delays absorption of venom into the circulation, is recommended in such cases (but not after bites by other species). The entire bitten limb is splinted and, as tightly as for a sprained ankle, bandaged with a 4.5 m long, 10 cm wide crepe bandage, starting at the fingers or toes and proceeding proximally. Early anaphylactic reactions should be treated with epinephrine (adrenaline) (doses below).

Hospital treatment
Clinical assessment
Unless the snake responsible was definitely a non-venomous species, the victim should be admitted to hospital for at least 24 hours' observation.

Antivenom
Antivenom, the only specific antidote to snake venoms, is IgG raised in horses or sheep by immunisation with one or more venoms and refined to $F(ab')_2$ or Fab fragments. In the management of a snake-bite victim, the most important decision is whether or not its use is indicated.

Indications for antivenom
Adder (Vipera berus) bites:
1. Sustained fall in blood pressure (systolic to <70 mmHg or by more than 50 mmHg below the normal or admission value confirmed by repeated measurements over 10-15 minutes) or other signs of shock;
2. Other features of systemic envenoming (see above), vomiting, spontaneous bleeding, haematuria, coagulopathy, pulmonary oedema or haemorrhage, ECG abnormalities, marked neutrophil leucocytosis or raised serum enzymes; *or*
3. Severe local envenoming: swelling extending up to or beyond the elbow or knee within six hours of the bite and, in adults, swelling extending beyond the wrist or ankle within four hours of the bite.

Additional indications for antivenom after bites by exotic snakes:
1. Neurotoxicity;
2. Generalized rhabdomyolysis; *or*
3. Severe local envenoming: rapid extension of local swelling, especially after bites by species known to have necrotic venoms, and swelling of more than half the bitten limb developing within 48 hours of the bite.

Administration of antivenom

Skin and conjunctival 'hypersensitivity' tests do not predict early (anaphylactoid) or late (serum sickness type) antivenom reactions. Patients at high risk of antivenom reactions (ie, atopic subjects and those who have had previous reactions to equine/ovine serum) should be premedicated with subcutaneous epinephrine (adrenaline), antihistamine and a corticosteroid (doses below).

For adder bites, use European Viper Venom Serum (Zagreb, available from Farillon). For exotic species consult the National Poisons Centre about urgent supply of an antivenom of appropriate specificity. Ideally, antivenom should be given as soon as indicated (see specific clinical indications listed above) but, as it can reverse systemic envenoming by exotic snakes even several days after the bite, antivenom is indicated whenever systemic signs are present.

Intravenous administration is the most effective, either by infusion - diluted in approximately 5 ml of 0.9% sodium chloride/kg body weight (which is easier to control) - or by intravenous 'push' injection of undiluted antivenom (2 mL/min). The incidence and severity of reactions is the same with these two methods.

Dose of antivenom

For adder bites, the initial dose is one vial (10 mL) of Zagreb antivenom, which can be repeated after one to two hours if shock, vomiting or anaphylactoid symptoms persist or recur. For exotic snake-bites, the initial dose will vary with the species of snake, type of antivenom and severity of envenoming (see Further Reading). **Children must be given the same dose as adults.**

Response to antivenom
There may be marked symptomatic improvement soon after treatment and blood pressure and consciousness may be restored. Spontaneous systemic bleeding usually stops within 15-30 minutes and blood coagulability is restored within six hours, provided that a neutralising dose has been given. The initial dose of antivenom should be repeated if severe signs of envenoming persist after one to two hours, or if blood coagulability is not restored within six hours. Systemic envenoming may recur hours or days after initially responding to antivenom, as a result of continuing absorption of venom from the bite site after the dose of antivenom has been cleared from the bloodstream. Envenomed patients should therefore be observed in hospital for at least three days.

Antivenom reactions
Early (anaphylactic/anaphylactoid) reactions develop within 30 minutes of starting antivenom. Symptoms include itching, urticaria, cough, nausea, vomiting, other autonomic manifestations, fever, hypotension, bronchospasm and angio-oedema. Death is rare but individual cases, such as a boy with asthma who died from anaphylactic shock after Pasteur antivenom in England in 1957, have been widely publicised and have led to an unreasonable rejection of antivenom treatment. Most reactions are not type I, IgE-mediated hypersensitivity reactions to equine/ovine serum protein, but are caused by complement activation by immune complexes, IgG aggregates or residual Fc fragments in the antivenom. Pyrogenic reactions are caused by endotoxin contamination. Fever, rigors, febrile convulsions in children, vasodilatation and a fall in blood pressure develop one to two hours after treatment.

Late reactions (serum sickness) may develop 5-24 (mean seven) days after antivenom. Clinical features include fever, itching, urticaria, arthralgia (including the temperomandibular joint), lymphadenopathy, periarticular swellings, mononeuritis multiplex and albuminuria.

Treatment of antivenom reactions

Epinephrine (adrenaline) is effective; initially 0.5 mL of 0.1% (1 in 1000, 1 mg/mL) by intramuscular injection to adults (children 0.01 mL/kg) at the first signs of a reaction, repeated after about five minutes if the reaction is not controlled. An H_1 antihistamine, such as chlorpheniramine maleate (10 mg for adults, 0.2 mg/kg for children) is given by slow intravenous injection to combat the effects of histamine released during the reaction. Pyrogenic reactions are treated by cooling the patient and giving antipyretics. Late reactions respond to an oral antihistamine such as chlorpheniramine (4 mg six-hourly for adults, 0.25 mg/kg/daily in divided doses for children) or to oral prednisolone (5 mg six-hourly for five to seven days for adults, 0.3 mg/kg/daily in divided doses for children).

Supportive treatment

1. *Bulbar and respiratory paralysis:* the airway must be maintained and assisted ventilation instituted as soon as respiratory distress develops. As some patients respond to anticholinesterases a 'Tensilon' test should be performed: atropine sulphate (0.6 mg for adults, 50 micrograms/kg for children) then edrophonium chloride (2 mg followed after 30 seconds if no adverse reaction has occurred by 8 mg for adults, 20 micrograms/kg followed by 80 micrograms/kg for children) given by intravenous injection. Treatment is continued with neostigmine methylsulphate in those who respond.

2. *Hypotension and shock*: hypovolaemia should be corrected. If this fails, dopamine or dobutamine should be tried.

3. *Oliguria and renal failure*: if urine flow fails to increase after cautious rehydration, diuretics and dopamine will be required. If conservative treatment fails, dialysis should be started.

4. *Local envenoming*: nurse the bitten limb in the most comfortable position. Surgical debridement and broad-spectrum antibiotics are indicated immediately if signs of local necrosis have developed.

Increased pressure within tight fascial compartments such as the digital pulp spaces and anterior tibial compartment may cause ischaemic damage but fasciotomy is appropriate only if the intracompartmental pressure exceeds 45 mmHg and blood coagulability has been restored.

Conclusions

- First aid measures after snake-bite should include immobilisation of the affected limb. After bites by neurotoxic elapids, crepe bandaging 'pressure immobilisation' is indicated.
- Local incision, suction and tourniquets are potentially harmful and should not be employed.
- Unless the snake responsible was definitely non-venomous the patient should be admitted to hospital for at least 24 hours' observation.
- Antivenom is the only specific antidote to snake venoms: indications for its use depend on careful clinical assessment.
- The dose of antivenom given to children is the same as the adult dose.
- A full range of supportive-care facilities is needed in many cases.

Contact telephone numbers

National Poisons
Information Centre   0171 635 9191

Professor DA Warrell/Dr David Lalloo
Telephone   01865 221332/220968/220279
Fax   01865 220984
E Mail   david.warrell@ndm.ox.ac.uk
Dr RDG Theakston   0151 708 9393

Further reading
Karlson-Stiber C, Persson H, Heath A, Smith D, Al-Abdulla IH, Sjöström L. First clinical experiences with specific sheep Fab fragments in snake bite: report of a

multicentre study of *Vipera berus* envenoming. *J Intern Med* 1997; **241:** 53-8.

Karlson-Stiber C, Persson H. Antivenom treatment in *Vipera berus* envenoming: report of 30 cases. *J Intern Med* 1994; **235:** 57-61.

Meier J, White J, eds. *Clinical toxicology of animal venoms*. Boca Raton: CRC Press, 1995.

Persson H, Irestedt B. A study of 136 cases of adder bite treated in Swedish hospitals during one year. *Acta Med Scand* 1981; **210:** 433-9.

Reid HA. Adder bites in Britain. *BMJ* 1976; **2:** 153-6.

Reid HA. Bites by foreign venomous snakes in Britain. *BMJ* 1978; **1:** 1598-1600.

Theakston RD, Warrell DA. Antivenoms: a list of hyperimmune sera currently available for the treatment of envenoming by bites and stings. *Toxicon* 1991; **29:** 1419-70.

Warrell DA. Venoms, toxins, and poisons of animals and plants. In: Weatherall DJ, Ledingham JGG, Warrell DA, eds. *Oxford textbook of medicine*. 3rd ed. Oxford: Oxford University Press, 1996; 1124-51. (vol 1).

Warrell DA. Animal toxins. In: Cook GC, ed. *Manson's tropical diseases*. London: WB Saunders 1996; 468-515.

Management of chronic lymphocytic leukaemia

Daniel Catovsky
Professor of Haematology
Academic Department of Haematology & Cytogenetics
Royal Marsden Hospita and Institute of Cancer Research
London SW3 6JJ

Introduction

Chronic lymphocytic leukaemia (CLL) is the most common leukaemia in adults aged 50 years and over; more than 1,000 new cases are seen annually in England and Wales. Although it is generally thought of as a benign disease it has, in fact, a very variable course: while some patients never require treatment, in others the disease is of short evolution and progressive course. The reason for this different clinical behaviour is not clear, but it may be related to cytogenetic changes and/or mutations in the p53 suppressor gene. The last decade has seen considerable progress in our understanding of the natural history of CLL and its clinical and morphological changes, as well as advances in treatment.

CLL affects twice as many male as female patients, with peak incidence between the ages of 60 and 80 years. However, in the 6% of patients below the age of 50 years, the disease tends to be more aggressive.

Diagnosis

CLL presents as a persistent lymphocytosis ($>10 \times 10^9$/L) with more than 30% lymphocytes in the bone marrow. A diagnosis can be made when counts are lower, if clonality by membrane immunoglobulins and other typical CLL markers are demonstrable. A raised lymphocyte count is a chance finding in at least one-third of patients; others may present with symptoms of nodal enlargement or, more rarely, anaemia, thrombocytopenia or with an infective episode.

Twenty years ago, most patients with lymphocytosis would have been labelled as having CLL without undergoing any other tests. It has since become apparent that there are many causes of lymphocytosis, chiefly other B-cell lymphoproliferative diseases, which are distinct from CLL[1]. The main tests for this differential diagnosis are cell markers, which can define the immunophenotype of the lymphocytes as of B- or T-cell lineage. Five monoclonal antibodies give a characteristic profile in CLL: weak immunoglobulin, positive CD5 and CD23 and negative FMC7 and CD79b. The same markers in other B-cell disorders show strong membrane immunoglobulin, negative CD5 and CD23 and positive CD79 and FMC7[2]. The only exception is mantle-cell lymphoma in which CD5 is positive, and this may be confused with CLL.

Peripheral blood and bone-marrow films show typical features in CLL, with marrow trephine biopsy showing interstitial or nodular infiltration in early stages of the disease and a packed pattern, with little residual haemopoiesis, at the advanced stage. Lymph-node biopsies are rarely necessary, but in patients who present with lymphadenopathy a biopsy may be the first available test.

Staging
A staging system was first proposed by Rai et al in 1975[3], based on physical examination and blood count. This represented significant progress because it showed that patients with minimal disease, no physical signs and no anaemia or thrombocytopenia had a longer survival than those who had anaemia or thrombocytopenia.

The Binet or International staging system, used more frequently in Europe, has three stages: A, B and C. Patients with stage A CLL (50-60% of cases) have no anaemia or thrombocytopenia and may have lymphadenopathy in one or two sites, usually bilateral in the neck or axillae. Patients with stage B disease (30%) have similar findings: haemoglobin >10 g/dl and platelets >100x10^9/l, and three or more sites of nodal enlargement - eg, neck, axillae, groins (the spleen is also considered a nodal site). In patients with stage C disease (up to 20%), the haemoglobin concentration is below 10 g/dl and/or the platelet level below 100x10^9/l. Chest X-rays and abdominal computed tomography (CT) scans are often used to assess nodal involvement and, although this information is not included in either staging system, imaging investigations are useful in assessment of treatment response.

Prognostic factors

Stage is the most important factor but other disease features should also be considered. For example, a lymphocyte doubling time of less than one year in patients with stage A disease carries a poor prognosis and is associated with a progressive course. Age is also important with younger patients, even with more aggressive disease, surviving longer than older ones. It is worth noting that in about 50% of patients with stage A disease, the cause of death is not related to CLL[4].

The prognosis is likely to be better in patients with stages B and C disease who respond to primary treatment than in those who do not, but the outlook improves in those responding to second-line therapy. It is poor in those refractory to all treatments.

Although any degree of response is better than none, the prognosis is better in patients with complete remission (normalisation of the bone-marrow findings and blood counts and regression of physical signs) than in those with a partial or minimal response. Studies in the United Kingdom[4] have shown that survival is better overall in women, possibly for multifactorial reasons; the disease tends to be more benign, and women tend to respond better to treatment.

Treatment strategies

Trials in France and the UK have shown that survival does not improve when patients with stage A CLL are treated and that, in fact, they seem to fare worse[5]. The current indications for treatment are, consequently, stage B and C disease, where patients usually display symptoms and evidence of progression.

Several drugs are effective in the treatment of CLL. In patients presenting with anaemia or thrombocytopenia (stage C), once the possibility of folate or B_{12} deficiency or autoantibodies has been excluded, the first objective is to improve bone-marrow function. One of the best measures is to use a single corticosteroid for four to six weeks, which often improves blood count and facilitates subsequent management.

Prednisolone used at 40-50 mg daily may artificially induce a higher degree of lymphocytosis and, at the same time, improve the haemoglobin and platelet levels and reduce the size of lymph nodes and spleen. This effect lasts a few weeks and is usually followed by a gradual reduction in the lymphocyte count, due to the powerful lympholytic effect of corticosteroids. Giving them in pulses intermittently with the alkylating agents chlorambucil or cyclophosphamide, or as part of the combination COP (cyclophosphamide, vincristine, prednisone), shows no advantage over using alkylating agents alone. Corticosteroids are recommended on a more prolonged basis for patients with haemolytic anaemia (5-10% of patients) or immune thrombocytopenia (1-2%). Patients refractory to treatment may respond to very-high-dose corticosteroids - eg, methylprednisolone at $1g/m^2$ in pulses of five days each month. It is important for patients with CLL who are receiving prolonged treatment with corticosteroids to be given histamine$_2$-blockers and antifungal prophylaxis - eg, oral nystatin or fluconazole.

For many years the mainstay of treatment for CLL patients has been the alkylating agents and, of these, chlorambucil (in use since the 1960s) is the most popular. It has been used continuously at a low dose (eg, 2-4 mg daily) but, in the last ten years, higher doses have been used intermittently. The Medical Research Council (MRC) CLL trial recommends a dose of 10 mg/m^2 for six days each month for up to one year. If there is little evidence of response after three to four months, treatment should be discontinued and alternative therapy considered. In previously untreated patients the complete remission rate with chlorambucil is 10-15% and the partial remission rate around 60%. There is some evidence that chlorambucil could be used at even higher doses over longer periods in which case the response rate may be higher, but myelosuppression is increased. Significant neutropenia and thrombocytopenia are seen in 20% of patients treated with chlorambucil.

National and international trials have examined the value of giving anthracyclines such as doxorubicin, in addition to alkylating agents. The French Co-operative Group suggested that the combination CHOP (cyclophosphamide, doxorubicin, vincristine and prednisone) is better than chlorambucil for stage C CLL. Patients in the MRC CLL3 trial have received either chlorambucil or chlorambucil plus epirubicin, but results are not yet available. However, the results of large overviews and published reports indicate that, whilst the addition of anthracyclines may increase the response rate, the overall effect on survival has yet to be determined.

New trials focus on the nucleoside analogues, of which fludarabine is the most important in CLL[6,7]. This group also includes cladribine and pentostatin which have shown activity in other low-grade malignancies, chiefly hairy-cell leukaemia. Fludarabine produces a higher overall response rate than chlorambucil, and the question arises as to whether fludarabine should be used as first-line therapy or remain as second-line treatment for non-responders. A complete remission rate of 15-20% and a partial remission rate of 50-60% can be obtained with fludarabine in patients resistant to alkylating agents, the response rate in previously untreated patients being higher[6]; whether the improved response rate with fludarabine translates to a prolonged survival is unclear.

Despite its apparent benefits the use of fludarabine is associated with a higher complication rate as it is myelotoxic, neutropenia being seen in 50% and thrombocytopenia in 30% of previously treated patients. In 5-10% of patients, fludarabine may precipitate autoimmune haemolytic anaemia above the baseline rate seen in CLL.

Cladribine has been reported to lead to equally good remission rates but its dosage and treatment protocol have not been optimised for CLL. The rate of thrombocytopenia and infectious complications may be higher and the response duration shorter than with fludarabine, which is given at a dose of 25mg/m^2 intravenously daily for five days repeated every four weeks until maximum response is reached, usually after four to six courses. The better the response achieved, the longer will be the subsequent disease-free period. Fludaribine is now being considered for patients less than 55 years of age, in whom achievement of complete remission may be a pre-condition for high-dose therapy which is followed by autologous transplantation.

Prevention and management of infections
The low serum immunoglobulin levels and cytopenias associated with therapy predispose patients with CLL to recurrent infections, particularly of the respiratory tract, and the role of GPs in the management of infection is crucial. Patients should be advised about the prompt use of broad-spectrum antibiotics and we suggest that patients keep a supply of (for example) amoxycillin, co-amoxiclav or clarithromycin, and initiate treatment immediately if they develop upper respiratory symptoms or a fever. Patients treated with fludarabine require prophylaxis with co-trimoxazole to prevent *Pneumocystis carinii* infection which has been reported in patients receiving corticosteroids. Those with repeated infections relating to low immunoglobulin levels may benefit from intravenous infusions of gammaglobulin - eg, 12-18 g - on a monthly basis during the winter months. Although antibody responses are not good in patients with CLL, it is advisable for them to be immunised regularly against influenza and possibly against pneumococcal infections. Patients with CLL may take longer to respond

so we advise antibiotic courses of seven to ten days, in contrast to the standard five days.

Conclusions

- Interest in CLL has increased, due to evidence suggesting that its incidence may be increasing with the life-span of the population.
- It can now be diagnosed more precisely, and the likely prognosis estimated, from simple clinical findings and a full blood count.
- Research is in progress to identify why CLL is more aggressive in some patients and to throw light on pathogenesis, which may lead to new treatments.
- Agents currently available have widened the range of therapeutic options and have led to better patient care.

References

1. Catovsky D. Chronic lymphocytic leukaemia and other leukaemias of mature B and T cells. In: Weatherall D, Ledingham JGG, Warreld DA, eds. *Oxford textbook of medicine*. 3rd ed. Oxford: Oxford University Press, 1995; 3419-25 (vol 3).
2. Moreau E, Matutes E, A'Hern R, et al. Improvement of the chronic lymphocytic leukaemia scoring system with the monoclonal antibody SN8 (CD79b). *Am J Clin Pathol* 1997; **108:** 378-82.
3. Rai KR, Sawitsky A, Cronkite E, Chanana AD, Levy RN, Pasternack BS. Clinical staging of chronic lymphocytic leukaemia. *Blood* 1975; **46:** 219-34.
4. Catovsky D, Fooks J, Richards S. Prognostic factors in chronic lymphocytic leukaemia: the importance of age, sex and response to treatment in survival: a report from the MRC CLL 1 trial. *Br J Haematol* 1989; **72:** 141-9.
5. French Cooperative Group on Chronic Lymphocytic Leukaemia. Natural history of stage A chronic lymphocytic leukaemia: untreated patients. *Br J Haematol* 1990; **76**: 45-57.
6. Keating MJ, O'Brien S, Kantarjian H, et al. Long-term follow-up of patients with chronic lymphocytic leukemia treated with fludarabine as a single agent. *Blood* 1993; **81:** 2878-84.
7. Johnson S, Smith AG, Loffler H, et al. Multicentre prospective randomised trial of fludarabine versus cyclophosphamide, doxorubicin, and prednisone (CAP) for treatment of advanced-stage chronic lymphocytic leukaemia. *Lancet* 1996; **347**: 1432-8.

Analgesia for labour

Felicity Reynolds
Emeritus Professor of Obstetric Analgesia
United Medical and Dental Schools
of Guy's and St Thomas's Hospital
London SE1 7EH

Introduction

Labour pain is usually severe but readily forgotten, and there is a tendency to deny the need for pain relief. Many first-time mothers come ill-prepared for the pain of labour.

There are many approaches to analgesia in labour: a few relieve pain, some have a distracting or calming effect, some are actually detrimental and many have not been properly evaluated. With the development of inhalational anaesthetics in the mid 19th Century, ether, chloroform and nitrous oxide were used for labour analgesia - indeed Queen Victoria, on receiving chloroform for the birth of her eighth child (an early within-patient cross-over trial), pronounced it a "blessed relief". Truly painless childbirth, in the form of epidural analgesia, began to be a practical proposition in the 1970s but despite its lack of systemic effect for both mother and baby, and steady improvements in technique, it remains a minority method used by about 25% of mothers in the United Kingdom UK).

Non-pharmacological methods

A mother can benefit from antenatal training provided it engenders calm and relaxation, thus conserving energy, but it should be explained that she cannot *choose* to have an uncomplicated labour without the need for analgesia or other intervention. False expectations may induce distrust of caregivers, unwarranted feelings of failure when problems arise, and resentment when pain is encountered.

Psychological methods

These comprise preparation for childbirth in various forms, psychoprophylaxis, hypnosis and support by midwife, partner or doula (a supportive companion usually previously unknown to the mother) and are claimed to reduce the need for pharmacological analgesia and obstetric intervention. Randomised trials confirm this contention for support by a trained caregiver[1], but not for hypnosis which significantly *prolonged* labour[2]. It was found that prepared childbirth classes failed to reduce the demand for epidural analgesia[3]. Training probably provides a model for maternal self-control during labour, rather than a means of relieving pain.

Physical methods

These include warm water, massage, transcutaneous electrical nerve stimulation (TENS) and the less frequently used acupuncture, aromatherapy, audioanalgesia, biofeedback and reflexology. Efficacy is unsupported by randomised trials and the only method to be well studied, TENS, is disappointing, particularly in late labour[4].

Homoeopathy and herbalism are often classed as 'non-pharmacological' methods. Again, scientific evidence for their efficacy is lacking.

All these methods depend to a large measure on distraction and, while mainly harmless, most require a substantial input from an enthusiastic instructor and are not widely applicable.

Systemic opioid analgesia

The synthetic opioid pethidine was legalised for use by midwives in 1950, in the surprising expectation that it would be free from the detrimental effects of morphine, namely sedation, nausea, and respiratory depression in the mother and her newborn child. In fact, neither drug reduces the pain score in labour[5,6] but both produce considerable sedation. Pethidine increases nausea and vomiting, which require administration of an anti-emetic such as metoclopramide. Many women feel disoriented and experience loss of control, though some find they mind pain less[4]. Maternal satisfaction can be improved by using patient-controlled administration. There is delayed gastric emptying, making general anaesthesia more dangerous. Babies may be rendered drowsy, so they should be given the opioid antagonist naloxone. There is little or no published evidence that alternatives such as meptazinol and nalbuphine have any advantages over pethidine. Diamorphine, which is popular in a few centres, particularly in Scotland, has yet to be evaluated scientifically.

Inhalational analgesia

During this century, nitrous oxide replaced ether and chloroform for labour analgesia as there was less danger of producing full anaesthesia, and it came to be realised that by limiting the inhaled concentration it was safe for self-administration. 'Entonox', a mixture of 50% nitrous oxide and 50% oxygen supplied either piped or in a cylinder with a demand valve, is now the most widely used analgesic in labour[4]. It is probably more effective overall than pethidine[4,7] though it has little effect on pain score and, again, may make women feel light-headed and nauseated. Maternal hyperventilation, in an effort to maximise analgesia, may induce dizziness and, over a prolonged period, alkalosis, which can impair placental respiratory gas exchange. Its efficacy may be enhanced by adding a low concentration of volatile agent such as isoflurane, but at the cost of greater drowsiness.

Regional analgesia

Epidural and (more rarely) spinal anaesthesia are used in labour to block pain from the uterus and birth canal. Paracervical block, rarely used in the UK, produces only uterine analgesia, while pudendal block affects only the birth canal.

Epidural analgesia involves administering local anaesthetic through a catheter in the area surrounding the dural sac to block the lower thoracic nerves for uterine pain and the sacral nerves for outlet pain. Initially, high concentrations of local anaesthetic were used and once bupivacaine became available excellent analgesia could be provided, but at the cost of progressive motor block and occasional hypotension. Adverse effects may be minimised by the addition of an opioid such as fentanyl, which potentiates analgesia, allowing bupivacaine dosage to be reduced, thus permitting mobility, and by use of larger volumes of more dilute solutions which improve spread.

An anaesthetist should site the catheter and give the first dose after which either bolus doses are given as required, generally by a midwife, or an infusion is used. Infusions reduce fluctuations in anaesthetic effect and the danger of hypotension and of mistakes, but increase dose requirement and the risk of motor block.

Advantages
Regional blockade is the only form of labour analgesia to produce a consistent reduction in pain score[6] without drowsiness, reducing the stress of labour with its attendant rise in catecholamines and deteriorating acid-base status. This is particularly beneficial in prolonged labour, or in the presence of maternal disease, multiple pregnancy, or a small or distressed fetus[8] and the baby tends to be in better condition after delivery.

Epidural analgesia is indicated in high-risk labour also because it can readily be intensified to allow surgery, thereby avoiding the risks associated with general anaesthesia.

Disadvantages and risks
Regional analgesia is labour-intensive, hence expensive, and the skill necessary to provide the service and to avoid dural puncture is not always available. Accidental dural puncture may result in a post-partum headache that is relieved by lying down. Neglect of this symptom can result in long-term morbidity and even mortality, so it requires urgent referral to an anaesthetist who can correct it with an epidural blood patch[9]. An intravenous infusion is needed to guard against hypotension. The second stage of labour is prolonged, but without detriment to the baby.

Accidental intravenous or subarachnoid injection with large doses of local anaesthetic can cause convulsions, excessive block and occasionally death, although low dose opioid/local anaesthetic combinations avoid this danger. Epidural opioids cause itching, but severe respiratory depression arises during labour only if they are used in conjunction with systemic opioids or other sedatives. Regional analgesia should not be used in the presence of a clotting disorder, as bleeding into the epidural space may cause root or cord compression.

Popular misconceptions
Epidurals are thought by some to cause backache and paralysis and to increase the need for caesarean section. However backache, common in pregnancy, often continues post partum and prospective studies consistently show that epidurals do not increase the incidence of chronic backache[10]. In fact, neurological sequelae are about six times more likely to result from childbirth itself than from regional block[11]. Transient paraesthesiae may follow root trauma, but my view is that serious sequelae do not occur without important errors of technique. American women who have had epidural analgesia may be more likely to be delivered by caesarean section, but this does not seem to be so in the UK.

Why is labour pain so resistant to methods of analgesia that are successful in other spheres? The answer is probably that it is not only intermittent but also exceedingly severe. The commonest complaints among mothers in a nationwide survey[4] were: why weren't they warned how bad it would be, and why were they deterred from requesting epidural analgesia until too late?

Conclusions
* The efficacy of the many non-pharmacological approaches to pain relief in labour is unsupported by evidence from randomised trials.
* Skilled support in labour is demonstrably beneficial, but most British women still request pharmacological analgesia.

- Of systemic agents, nitrous oxide is the best generally available; pethidine has several disadvantages including sedative rather than analgesic effects.
- Regional blockade alone can reliably reduce pain but it is expensive, requires skill and is not universally available.
- Regional blockade is particularly valuable for prolonged or complicated labour and for caesarean section.
- Combination of relatively low doses of a local anaesthetic and an opioid is safest and allows mobility.
- In a maternity unit, a skilled anaesthetist should always be available, and accidental dural puncture should be rare.

References

1. Update Software Ltd. *The Cochrane pregnancy and childbirth database*. Oxford: Update Software Ltd, 1993 (issue 1).
2. Freeman RM, Macaulay AJ, Eve L, Chamberlain GV, Bhat AV. Randomised trial of self hypnosis for analgesia in labour. *BMJ* 1986; **292:** 657-8.
3. Melzack R, Taenzer P, Feldman P, Kinch RA. Labour is still painful after prepared childbirth training. *Can Med Assoc J* 1981; **125:** 357-63.
4. Chamberlain G, Wraight A, Steer P. *Pain and its relief in childbirth: report of the 1990 NBT survey*. Edinburgh: Churchill Livingstone, 1993.
5. Olofsson C, Ekblom A, Ekman-Ordeberg G, Hjelm A, Irested TL. Lack of analgesic effect of systemically administered morphine or pethidine on labour pain. *Br J Obstet Gynaecol* 1996; **103:** 968-72.
6. Ranta P, Jouppila P, Spalding M, Kangas-Saarela, Hollmen A, Jouppila R. Parturients' assessment of water blocks, pethidine, nitrous oxide, paracervical and epidural blocks in labour. *Int J Obstet Anesth* 1994; **3:** 193-8.
7. Holdcroft A, Morgan M. An assessment of the analgesic effect in labour of pethidine and 50 per cent nitrous oxide in oxygen (Entonox). *J Obstet Gynaecol Br Commonw* 1974; **81:** 603-7.
8. Reynolds F, ed. *Effects on the baby of maternal analgesia and anaesthesia*. London: WB Saunders, 1993.
9. Reynolds F. Dural puncture and headache. *BMJ* 1993; **306:** 874-6.
10. Russell R, Dundas R, Reynolds F. Long term backache after childbirth: prospective search for causative factors. *BMJ* 1996; **312:** 1384-8.
11. Holdcroft A, Gibberd FB, Hargrove RL, Hawkins DF, Dellaportas CI. Neurological complications associated with pregnancy. *Br J Anaesth* 1995; **75:** 522-6.

Symptom control in terminal illness

Christina Faull
Consultant in palliative care
St. Mary's Hospice
Birmingham B29 7DA

Introduction

This article will discuss the pharmacological management of some of the common physical symptoms, other than pain, arising in terminal illness. Many of the management strategies discussed below describe the use of drugs outside their licensed indications, but such uses are established and accepted good practice. Physical symptom management is only one dimension of good palliative care, and a multiprofessional team is important in achieving good control of physical and non-physical symptoms alike.

General principles

When a disease is advanced and cure and remission are no longer possible, enhancement of the quality of life of the patient must be the main focus of care. The health care team must know the problems as the *patient* sees them and understand his or her priorities and wishes; there must be very clear communication with the patient concerning that individual's personal cost-benefit ratio of any proposed treatments. Optimal management of symptoms relies on anticipation, assessment of likely causes and the effects on the patient and family, explanation, close supervision and re-evaluation[1]. Removal of the underlying cause of symptoms provides the best palliation, but for many patients with advanced illness this may be neither possible nor appropriate.

Fatigue and anorexia

These symptoms are a major cause of concern to patients and their carers. They are interlinked since insufficient nutrition inevitably leads to fatigue. Table 1 sets out potentially reversible causes.

Table 1: *Potentially reversible causes of fatigue and anorexia*

Fatigue	Anorexia
Hypocortisolism	Nausea
Electrolyte imbalance	Constipation
Hypotension	Dry mouth
Drugs - opioids	Oro-oesophageal thrush
- hypotensives	Drugs

Management

Dietetic and occupational therapy advice is valuable. Corticosteroids have been show to have a potent but short-lived effect on appetite[2]- dexamethasone 4 mg daily having less mineralocorticoid effect than prednisolone. Progestogens at high doses increase appetite and allow weight gain[3] although, as their effect is relatively slow, they will not be useful for patients who have weeks rather than months to live. Alcohol may also have a role in appetite stimulation.

Nausea and vomiting

Understanding the cause facilitates a logical approach to treatment and selection of a first-line antiemetic (see Table 2); if this fails, a change should be made to an antiemetic with a different or broader spectrum of neurotransmitter activity. Some patients require co-administration of two antiemetics (with different neurotransmitter activity) to control nausea. The best route of drug delivery should be carefully considered.

Table 2: *Uses of antiemetic drugs*

Neurotransmitter activity	Potential use	Drug	Route
Antidopaminergic	Biochemical and drug-induced nausea	Haloperidol Prochlorperazine	o, s/c, i/v, i/m o, p/r, buccal, i/v, i/m
	As above, plus gastric statis Squashed stomach syndrome	Metoclopramide Domperidone	o, s/c, i/v, i/m o, p/r
Antihistamine and anticholinergic	Nausea related to: movement raised intracranial pressure gastrointestinal stimulation (vagal afferent) Nausea of unclear origin	Cyclizine	o, s/c, i/m
Anticholinergic	Nausea related to movement	Hyoscine hydrobromide	o, s/c, i/m, i/v
Antiserotoninergic	Emesis related to chemotherapy	Ondansetron Granisetron	o, i/v o, i/v
Broad spectrum	Nausea of unclear origin	Methotrimeprazine	o, s/c, i/m
Uncertain	Chemotherapy Adjunct in nausea of unclear origin	Corticosteroids	o, i/v, s/c, i/m

o = oral, s/c = subcutaneous, i/v = intravenous, i/m = intramuscular, p/r = per rectum

Intestinal obstruction.

While surgical management should always be considered, it may be neither possible nor desirable in patients with advanced cancer. Medical management may allow patients to be cared for at home (see Table 3)[4]. As drugs should not be given orally, a subcutaneous infusion pump is generally used.

Table 3: *Measures for intestinal obstruction*

Intervention	Drugs
Reduce colic	Hyoscine butylbromide 60-120 mg/day s/c Stop laxatives and prokinetic drugs
Reduce discomfort from distension	Diamorphine s/c (to replace oral morphine at 1/3 dose)
Reduce nausea	Cyclizine 50-200 mg/day and/or haloperidol 3-10 mg/day
Reduce intestinal secretions	Hyoscine butylbromide 60-120 mg/day Omeprazole 20 mg once or twice daily If above treatment fails, Octreotide 50-600 microgrammes/day (start high and reduce to lowest effective dose or stop if ineffective)[5] Nasogastric tube
Reduce thirst	Free access to ice and drinks Attention to mouth care I/v or s/c fluids

s/c = subcutaneous, i/v = intravenous

Some vomiting may still occur but, if nausea is controlled, this is generally tolerable. A nasogastric tube and parenteral fluids may occasionally be useful but are not always desired by patients. In subacute, incomplete obstruction a trial infusion of metoclopramide (30-120 mg daily) and dexamethasone (4-12 mg daily) may enhance kinesis.

Constipation

Constipation should be anticipated in all patients prescribed weak or strong opioids or anticholinergic drugs, and stimulant laxatives should be prescribed concurrently. These include senna and bisacodyl; combined stimulant and softeners include co-danthrusate and co-danthromer. The dose of laxative should be increased as the opioid dose increases.

Reduced activity and poor fluid and fibre intake in patients with advanced disease, in addition to specific drug adverse effects, make constipation a very common problem and 25% of patients treated with oral laxatives require intermittent use of enemas and suppositories.

Cough

Treatment for a dry cough

Demulcents contain soothing substances such as syrup or glycerol. Their effect is short-lived and there is no evidence to suggest that compound preparations offer any advantage over simple linctus (5 mL three to four times daily). Opioids work primarily by suppressing the cough reflex. Codeine linctus 5-10 mL three to four times daily should be used rather than a compound preparation: if codeine is ineffective a strong opioid such as morphine or methadone should be used. However, if a patient is already receiving a strong opioid for pain relief there is no logic in adding codeine, methadone or other opioid as a separate cough suppressant.

Nebulised local anaesthetics are occasionally used in specialist centres, but their use is limited by their unpleasant taste, oropharyngeal numbness, risk of aspiration and bronchoconstriction and a short duration of action (10-30 minutes). Suggested doses are 2% lignocaine (5 mL) or 0.25% bupivacaine (5 mL) three to four times daily. A test dose should always be given under close observation to ensure bronchospasm or other adverse effects are rapidly treated.

Treatment for a productive cough

The expectoration of mucus may be encouraged by physiotherapy, steam inhalations and nebulised 0.9% saline (2.5 mL-5 mL); nebulised acetylcysteine may sometimes be more effective. Some individual patients benefit from oral mucolytics (eg, acetylcysteine 200 mg orally three times daily).

A productive cough distressing a dying patient who is too weak to expectorate should be suppressed.

Breathlessness
Symptomatic management

Opioids diminish ventilatory drive and morphine can reduce breathlessness at rest. Patients not already treated with opiates should receive small doses initially (eg, 2.5 mg oral morphine four to six times daily), the dose and dose interval titrated according to response and side-effects. In patients already receiving opiates, the dose should be increased in steps of 30-50%, as tolerated and effective. A continuous subcutaneous infusion of opiate may be better tolerated and more effective, possibly by avoiding the peaks (with side-effects) and troughs (with loss of effect) of oral medication.

Oxygen should be available to severely hypoxic patients. In those with less severe hypoxia, a trial of oxygen therapy can be given via nasal prongs.

Benzodiazepines and other anxiolytics may be useful in anxious patients - eg, diazepam initially 2-5 mg three times daily reducing over several days to a maintenance dose of 2-5 mg at night.

Terminal restlessness and agitation

In the terminal phase of their illness many patients become agitated and confused[6]; the reasons for this are often unclear but may include hypotension, hypoxia, biochemical abnormalities and urinary retention. Midazolam (2.5-5 mg as a single subcutaneous dose, or as an infusion of 5-30 mg daily), methotrimeprazine (12.5-50 mg as a single subcutaneous dose, or as an infusion of 12.5-100 mg daily) or diazepam (as a 5-10 mg suppository) may be useful.

Conclusions

- A multiprofessional team is important in achieving good control of physical and non-physical symptoms.
- Enhancement of the patient's quality of life and death should be the main focus of care.
- Although it is always possible to help a patient, it is not always possible to relieve symptoms completely, but adequate relief of the patient's distress must be achieved. Specific help may be needed.
- The best route of drug administration should be carefully considered.
- Attention to detail is paramount.

Acknowledgements

Some of this work is based on *Guidelines for the use of drugs in symptom control in palliative care* produced by the West Midlands Palliative Care Physicians and Department of Medicines Management, Keele University, and adapted from: Faull C, Carter Y, Woof R eds. *Handbook of palliative care*. Oxford: Blackwell Science (in press).

References

1. Twycross R. *Introducing palliative care*. Oxford: Radcliffe Medical Press, 1995; 63-7.
2. Twycross R. Corticosteroids in advanced cancer. *BMJ* 1992; **305:** 969-70.
3. Davis CL, Hardy JR. Palliative care. *BMJ* 1994; **308:** 1359-62.
4. Ripamonti C, De Conno F, Ventafridda V, Rossi B, Baines MJ. Management of bowel obstruction in advanced and terminal cancer patients. *Ann Oncol* 1993; **4:** 15-21.

5. Riley J, Fallon MT. Octreotide in terminal malignant obstruction of the gastrointestinal tract. *Eur J Pall Care*; **1**: 23-5.
6. Back, IN. Terminal restlessness in patients with advanced malignant disease. *Palliat Med* 1992; **6**: 293-8.

Prescribers' Journal Committee of Management

The Department of Health (DH) invites applications from general practitioners, practising in the National Health Service, to fill three vacancies on this Committee from Summer 1998. Appointments are usually tenable for four years.

Meetings take place in London on the second Thursday afternoon of each calendar month, to assess and plan articles for *Prescribers' Journal*.

The Committee is independent and accountable to the Chief Medical Officer. DH, which has ultimate responsibility for management aspects, is an equal opportunities employer and welcomes applications for these posts regardless of gender, race, disability or sexuality. Appointments will be made on merit, based on the knowledge, skills, experience and personal qualities of the people concerned. All applicants will be required to provide the names of three independent referees. Nominations by institutions, rather than by the individual concerned, should be accompanied by written evidence that the individual is aware of, and agreeable to, such a nomination. No payments are made for such membership of this Committee, although allowable expenses under DH regulations would be met.

A job description and list of skills/qualities needed will be sent on written request. Nominations and/or inquiries should be sent to the Medical Editorial Unit of the Department of Health at: Box PJCOMAD.981, Room 122 Eileen House, 80-94 Newington Causeway, London SE1 6EF (fax: 0171 972 1079). The closing date for applications is Thursday 16 April 1998.

Spasticity after stroke

A Peter Moore
Senior Lecturer in Neurology
University of Liverpool
Walton Centre for Neurology and Neurosurgery
Liverpool L9 1AE

Introduction

Spasticity is only one of many impairments which can hinder recovery after stroke[1], and is important both because it is usually treatable and because treatment can be costly. It is a clinical syndrome of excessive and inappropriate involuntary muscle activity, usually combined with weakness of voluntary movements and other features of upper motor neurone dysfunction. There may be muscle stiffness, increased tendon reflexes, spasms, pain, limb posturing and deformity. Spasticity commonly impedes voluntary movements and nursing, contributes to secondary complications such as pressure sores, and can be unsightly. However, spasticity is sometimes useful, for example leg extensor spasticity can aid walking or transfers.

Scale of the problem

In the United Kingdom, service provision is based on a prevalence of stroke of some 500-800 per 100,000 population, but the true figure may be higher. About 100,000 patients have a first stroke every year: 20-30% die in the first month, and 15% of survivors die each subsequent year. About 25% of patients admitted to hospital become permanently institutionalised. It is not clear how many survivors develop clinically important spasticity, and eventual disability may depend on treatment in the early stages.

Pathogenesis

Spasticity is detected clinically by an increased resistance to passive stretch. Although this is traditionally ascribed to reflex hyperexcitability (the neural component), many patients with clinical spasticity do not have hyper-reflexia[2]. Biomechanical factors are probably equally important, such as reduced muscle compliance (stiffness) due to soft tissue changes, muscle contracture (shortening), and joint stiffness. These biomechanical changes may also potentiate the stretch reflex.

There is increasing evidence that maintaining stretch can minimise contractures as the soft tissue changes appear to develop only in muscles which are allowed to remain short.

Natural history and prediction of spasticity

The development of spasticity and its response to treatment are unpredictable. Its onset is highly variable, and the biomechanical and neural components can evolve at different times; for instance, muscle shortening may emerge from the acute flaccid paralysis within a few days, while brisk reflexes may take months to appear[2]. Spasticity can fluctuate dramatically with position, movement, fatigue, stress, drugs and even the weather. Following a typical hemiplegia, there is usually greater tone in the leg extensors, shoulder abductors, elbow and wrist flexors and pronators. Unchecked, this may lead rapidly to fully developed spasticity with contractures and secondary complications.

Aiding recovery - general principles

Starting treatment

The key is to have a clearly defined aim. Treatment is indicated to prevent secondary complications, to relieve pain, and to make nursing easier - for instance to aid hygiene, dressing and transferring, or to improve function. Effective treatment also has cosmetic benefits. Treatment should not be given if adverse effects of drugs are likely to outweigh any benefit or if spasticity is mild or functionally useful - eg, when it provides a helpful involuntary prop or brace to a weak limb. Thus patients who cannot stand can be treated more intensively than those who are still mobile.

Timing of intervention

Physical therapy should begin immediately. Muscle shortening may begin within days of a stroke, affecting flaccid muscles lying in a comfortable but shortened position for prolonged periods - eg, biceps with the arm resting in the lap, or calf muscles with the feet plantar-flexed. Once contractures and deformity develop they are very difficult to correct, and are likely to worsen as the neural component of spasticity appears, with brisk reflexes and muscle spasms which further impede stretching and positioning therapies. The intensity and duration of treatment must be individually tailored; patients may require anything from simple short-term measures to life-long intensive therapy. It is rarely too late to start treatment, but severe established spasticity and early spasticity require different therapy combinations. For example, it is unhelpful to give botulinum A toxin-haemagglutinin complex (BtA) to severely contracted muscles, but physiotherapy even four to five years after stroke can produce a modest but measurable improvement[3] although not necessarily due to direct treatment of spasticity.

Treatment of exacerbating factors

Especially in patients who cannot communicate, pain, poor positioning, infections, constipation, urinary retention, skin irritation or pressure sores can aggravate spasticity. Increasing spasticity can also signal other serious conditions such as a fractured limb or abdominal emergency.

Physical therapy

This includes proper positioning in bed and chair, stretching exercises, mobilisation, splints, casts and orthotic devices, and a variety of special measures - for example cold, ultrasound or other forms of heat may briefly relax a spastic muscle. Vibration, electrical stimulation or electromyograph biofeedback may have useful short-term effects and several dynamic physiotherapy methods can also help, although the relative merits of these special techniques are uncertain.

Positioning and seating

Poor positioning in the early stages after a stroke is a major cause of unnecessary spasticity and later deformity, and assiduous attention to correct positioning is essential. Attendants should aim to maintain stretch on spastic muscles to prevent contractures, and also experiment to find postures which minimise reflex hyperexcitability. Guidelines suggest that all joints should be put through a full range of movement on several occasions, totalling at least two hours a day[4], though this may not be practical in all situations. Also, passive stretching needs care since excessive force could promote fibrosis by damaging the muscle or the joint capsule. Once mobilised, proper seating should maintain a balanced, stable and symmetrical posture which is comfortable and maximises function.

Splints and casts

These can prevent or minimise the formation of contractures, and serial casting can improve the posture and range of movement in joints already contracted. Ankle-foot or wrist-finger splints are commonly helpful, though when spasticity is severe they may cause pressure sores which, in turn, aggravate the spasticity. The optimum duration of splinting is unclear.

Oral medication

Much of the published research showing benefit from drugs concerns spasticity due to primary spinal disease. By contrast, oral drugs are often disappointing in spasticity after stroke, although they may reduce painful flexor spasms and spontaneous clonus. Careful titration of the dose is essential as they may cause drowsiness, confusion and weakness, countering any benefit from reduced spasticity especially in the elderly; rapid withdrawal should also be avoided. However, single doses can give useful temporary control of spasticity before specific activities such as physiotherapy.

Baclofen is the most widely used agent. It is a centrally acting gamma-aminobutyric acid B-receptor agonist which should initially be given in divided doses of 15 mg per day, increasing up to 80 mg daily: larger doses are rarely more helpful. It can cause sedation or induce hallucinations and convulsions, particularly in the elderly or if the dose is increased too quickly. A paradoxical increase in spasticity can also occur.

Diazepam can be effective but is more likely to cause drowsiness and fatigue, and the overall benefit is small after stroke.

Dantrolene sodium can help, starting with a dosage of 25 mg daily and increasing up to 400 mg daily, in divided doses. It acts peripherally by inhibiting muscle excitation, but may still cause central adverse effects, and can also produce severe impairment of liver function.

Peripheral nerve blocks
The use of nerve blocks requires judgment and experience but they may help isolated or predominantly focal spasticity, and often reduce the need for oral medication. Nerve blocks weaken the muscle and reduce reflex excitability. They do not directly improve stiffness due to soft tissue or joint changes, but may abolish spasms and enable more effective use of antagonist muscles and maintenance of stretch. This allows easier positioning and helps to prevent or reduce contractures.

Neurolysis
Percutaneous perineural or intraneural injection with 2%-7% phenol or 50% alcohol damages nerve fibres and is used in a few centres to reduce severe spasticity in calf muscles (posterior tibial nerve), hip adductors (obturator), hamstrings (sciatic), biceps (musculocutaneous), and other muscles[5]. A preliminary trial of local anaesthetic may indicate the likely balance of weakness and reduction of spasticity. Injections can be acutely painful, and neurolysis of mixed motor/sensory nerves may cause persistent unpleasant or painful paraesthesiae. Controlled studies are needed to assess the place of these treatments.

Botulinum A toxin-haemagglutinin complex
Intramuscular injection of BtA selectively blocks the release of acetylcholine from the neuromuscular junction and weakens the muscle

for about three months. Proper use of physical therapies during this 'window' may prolong benefit. BtA can usefully reduce the impairment from focal arm or leg spasticity, but it is not yet clear whether this reduces the long-term disability after stroke[6]. Injections are relatively painless and have few or transient adverse effects, and BtA is easier to titrate than phenol/alcohol to preserve voluntary function. Its use in spasticity is increasing but it is not licensed for this condition and the risks and benefits following stroke have not been fully evaluated. It is expensive and commonly requires repeated treatments.

Surgical techniques
These can be considered in otherwise resistant cases and include anterior and posterior rhizotomy, lesions in the dorsal root entry zone (DREZ-otomy), and spinal cord and cerebellar stimulation. Osteotomy and tendon surgery may reduce otherwise fixed contractures or bony deformities.

Conclusions
- Spasticity after stroke has major resource implications. It is rarely an isolated problem, but is often treatable.
- A team approach and early treatment are essential to prevent contractures and other secondary complications.
- Physical therapies are most important, ensuring correct positioning of limbs and stretching of affected muscles.
- The use of botulinum toxin supplemented by local nerve blocks, low-dose oral medication or surgery is rarely needed.

References
1. Jeffery DR, Good DC. Rehabilitation of the stroke patient. *Curr Opin Neurol* 1995; **8**: 62-8.
2. O'Dwyer NJ, Ada L, Neilson PD. Spasticity and muscle contracture following stroke. *Brain* 1996; **119**: 1737-49.
3. Wade DT, Collen FM, Robb GF, Warlow CP. Physiotherapy intervention late after stroke and mobility. *BMJ* 1992; **304**: 609-13.
4. Development Trust for the Young Disabled. *The management of traumatic brain injury (report of the working party on the management of traumatic brain injury).* London: Medical Disability Society, 1988.

5. Skeil DA, Barnes MP. The local treatment of spasticity. *Clin Rehab* 1994; **8:** 240-6.

6. Bhakta BB, Cozens JA, Bamford JM, Chamberlain MA. Use of botulinum toxin in stroke patients with severe upper limb spasticity. *J Neurol Neurosurg Psychiatry* 1996; **61:** 30-5.

Minocycline-induced skin and tissue pigmentation

Clive B Archer
Consultant Dermatologist
University of Bristol, Department of Dermatology
Bristol Royal Infirmary
Bristol BS2 8HW

Introduction

Minocycline has similar antibacterial actions to other tetracyclines, but has been particularly promoted for the treatment of acne. Its adverse effects are similar to those of tetracycline and oxytetracycline, except that minocycline does not affect renal function. It causes dizziness and vertigo, and has been associated - rarely - with a lupus-like syndrome that can affect the lungs and liver[1]. In 4-15% of patients it causes skin pigmentation[2,3], which is considered here.

Clinical presentation

Three patterns of minocycline-induced skin pigmentation are recognised. They are of gradual onset, usually occurring after long-term use of the drug. Blue-black macular pigmentation is the commonest, localised to sites of inflammation or scarring such as acne lesions. Dermal pigment (often found free within macrophages) consisting of haemosiderin, ferritin or iron, chelated to minocycline or to a minocycline degradation product, is possibly responsible. Secondly, purplish, blue-black or slate-grey circumscribed macular pigmentation may be seen on the normal skin of the shins or arms[4,5]. Thirdly, a generalised muddy-brown pigmentation, accentuated in sun-exposed sites, can occur. Minocycline-induced pigmentary changes have also been reported, rarely, in the nails[6], sclerae[6,7], lips[8], oral mucosa[9,10] and teeth[6,9].

Predisposing factors

Minocycline-induced cutaneous pigmentation usually occurs after a high cumulative dose, although it has been reported after only three weeks' treatment (4.2 g total dose), suggesting a susceptibility in some individuals[11]. Pigmentary problems tend to be more prominent in older patients.

Differential diagnosis

Other causes of skin, eye and nail discolouration include argyria and pseudo-ochronosis induced by antimalarials. In addition, amiodarone and phenothiazines may cause slate-grey pigmentation of the sun-exposed sites, with sparing of the flexures and mucous membranes. Minocycline-induced pigmentation may also be confused with bruising, cyanosis, stasis dermatitis, persistent sun-tan and haemochromatosis.

Management

There is no specific treatment for pigmentation induced by minocycline, although laser therapy has been used experimentally. The drug should be withdrawn as soon as the adverse effect has been detected. At the sites of inflammation and scarring or of normal skin on the shins and arms, it usually fades over a period of years after discontinuation of therapy, whereas the diffuse pigmentation on sun-exposed areas tends to persist.

Prevention

Patients being considered for minocycline therapy should be warned about the possibility of pigmentary changes, and their physicians should monitor those on long-term therapy.

Conclusions

- Minocycline can cause blue-black, grey or brown skin pigmentation.
- Pigmentation is most likely in areas of inflammation or scarring.
- Treatment of long duration or at high dosage is most likely to cause pigmentation.
- Patients should be warned of this possible adverse effect of long-term treatment, and told to stop taking minocycline at the first sign of pigmentation.
- The pigmentation usually resolves over months or years, but can persist.

References

1. Gough A, Chapman S, Wagstaff K, Emery P, Elias E. Minocycline induced autoimmune hepatitis and systemic lupus erythematosus-like syndrome. *BMJ* 1996; **312:** 169-72.
2. Layton AM, Cunliffe WJ. Minocycline induced pigmentation in the treatment of acne - a review and personal observations. *J Dermatol Treat* 1989; **1:** 9-12.
3. Dwyer CM, Cuddihy AM, Kerr RE, Chapman RS, Allam BF. Skin pigmentation due to minocycline treatment of facial dermatoses. *Br J Dermatol* 1993; **129:** 158-62.
4. Argenyi ZB, Finelli L, Bergfeld WF, et al. Minocycline-related cutaneous hyperpigmentation as demonstrated by light microscopy, electron microscopy and X-ray energy spectroscopy. *J Cutan Pathol* 1987; **14:** 176-80.
5. Ridgway HA, Sonnex TS, Kennedy CT, Millard PR, Henderson WJ, Gold SC. Hyperpigmentation associated with oral minocycline. *Br J Dermatol* 1982; **107:** 95-102.
6. Wolfe ID, Reichmister J. Minocycline hyperpigmentation: skin, tooth, nail and bone involvement. *Cutis* 1984; **33:** 457-8.
7. Sabroe RA, Archer CB, Harlow D, Bradfield JW, Peachey RD. Minocycline-induced discolouration of the sclerae. *Br J Dermatol* 1996; **135:** 314-6.
8. Chu P, Van SL, Yen TS, Berger TG. Minocycline hyperpigmentation localized to the lips: an unusual fixed drug reaction? *J Am Acad Dermatol* 1994; **30:** 802-3.
9. Siller GM, Tod MA, Savage NW. Minocycline-induced oral pigmentation. *J Am Acad Dermatol* 1994; **30:** 350-4.
10. Eisen, D. Minocycline-induced oral hyperpigmentation. *Lancet* 1997; **349:** 400.
11. Fenske NA, Millns JL, Greer KE. Minocycline-induced pigmentation at sites of cutaneous inflammation. *JAMA* 1980; **244:** 1103-6.

Routes of drug administration:
7. Subcutaneous administration

Jeffrey K Aronson
Clinical Reader in Clinical Pharmacology
Radcliffe Infirmary
Oxford OX2 6HE

Introduction
Subcutaneous administration of drugs in man was first performed in 1836 by Lafargue, who introduced a paste of morphine under his own skin. The invention of the hypodermic syringe allowed, as its name suggests, subcutaneous injection, originally (by Wood in 1853) for local action, but later (by Hunter in 1858) for systemic effects.

Uses
Drugs may be administered subcutaneously for systemic action by injection, infusion, or implantation. Subcutaneous injection is used when a drug cannot be given orally, when the slow rate of diffusion of drug from the subcutaneous space is advantageous, or when the intravenous or intramuscular routes are contraindicated or disadvantageous. It is commonly used for vaccines, other compounds of large molecular weight (such as insulin, heparin, erythropoietin), interferons, and colony-stimulating factors (filgrastim, lenograstim, molgramostim). It is also used for apomorphine, which is poorly absorbed from the gut and causes serious adverse effects after oral administration, and for administering opioid analgesics and antiemetics in palliative care. Subcutaneous infusion (hypodermoclysis) is used for the administration of large volumes of fluid as an alternative to intravenous administration, particularly when intravenous access is limited or when administration needs to be prolonged; it can also be used

for continuous administration of drugs such as morphine, particularly in palliative care. Subcutaneous implantation of drugs such as goserelin, testosterone, and oestradiol is used to produce a prolonged effect with a single administration.

Advantages

Subcutaneous administration avoids the need for intravenous access, which can be technically difficult and carries risks of thrombophlebitis and infection. It also avoids the fluid overload and the need for frequent resiting of venous access that can complicate prolonged intravenous administration. Subcutaneous administration also avoids the disadvantages of intramuscular injection, including the risks of local reactions, nerve damage and haematoma formation[1]. It can easily be used by unskilled personnel, such as patients and their relatives or friends.

In the case of erythropoietin, the effective dosage is reduced by about 25% by subcutaneous compared with intravenous administration, and the fluctuation in therapeutic effect is less[2].

Absorption of drugs after subcutaneous injection

The drugs that are available for subcutaneous injection are generally completely absorbed from the subcutaneous tissues. Absorption occurs not only into the bloodstream, but also into the lymphatics; the clinical relevance of this is unclear. The rate of absorption of drugs after subcutaneous injection is slower than after a single intramuscular injection, although subcutaneous injection of a fine jet of solution, using a special pneumatically-driven 'gun', can increase the rate of absorption, without altering its overall extent.

Several factors affect the rate of absorption of a drug after subcutaneous injection[3]; for example:

Blood flow: the rate of absorption of insulin is increased by exercise of the limb into which the subcutaneous injection is given, and by an increase in the ambient temperature;

Site of injection: the absorption of insulin is faster from injection sites in the abdomen than in the arms, and much faster than in the legs;

Obesity: the rate of absorption is reduced as the amount of subcutaneous fat increases; *and*

The volume injected: the rate of absorption is slowed by increasing the volume of solution.

For most drugs these differences in rate of absorption are unimportant; they may affect short-term responses to insulin, but the effects of differences in long-term diabetic control are not known.

Injection technique

The preferred technique of single subcutaneous injection is to lift a fold of skin and insert the needle at an angle of 45°. This avoids inadvertent intramuscular injection in very thin individuals and children[4]. The alternative is to insert the needle at a right-angle, keeping the skin taut, the necessary technique when a pen injection device is used. It is probably unnecessary to swab the site before injection[5]. It is common to use a needle of gauge 25-27G, about 1-1.5 cm long (shorter needles are used with pen devices); a fine sharp needle minimises the pain of the injection. It is probably unnecessary to pull back on the syringe before injection; in one study of 204 injections no blood returned when that was done[4] and, in any case, injection is more likely to disrupt the skin capillaries than to result in intravascular administration. A volume of up to 2 mL per injection site can be used. Common sites of injection are over the deltoid muscles, the anterior thigh, the lateral abdomen between the ribs and the iliac crests, the chest below the clavicles and over the scapulae.

Adverse effects of single subcutaneous injections

Stinging or burning pain at the injection site is common with local anaesthetics, but is reportedly mitigated by the inclusion of sodium bicarbonate[6]. With subcutaneous heparin slight bruising is common.

Aseptic skin necrosis has occasionally been reported, particularly in the context of heparin-induced thrombocytopenia[7]. Other local adverse effects of subcutaneous injections are rare, although systemic adverse effects can occur. Lipodystrophies at the site of injection used to be common with insulin[8], but this is not the case with human insulin. Local infection (with *Mycobacterium avium* and *Clostridium septicum*) has been reported, rarely, in immunocompromised individuals.

Subcutaneous infusion ('hypodermoclysis')[9]

The subcutaneous compartment can accommodate large volumes of fluid during subcutaneous infusion, which can therefore be used as a means of hydration, for example following stroke or in palliative care. Isotonic saline (0.9% sodium chloride solution), glucose/saline (4% glucose/0.18% sodium chloride solution), or 5% glucose solution can be given this way, using gravity to drive the infusion at a rate of 75-150 mL/h to a maximum of 1-2 litres/day or 3 litres/day if two infusion sites are used. Hyaluronidase increases the rate of absorption but need only be used if very rapid administration is required, in which case 1,500 units of hyaluronidase and 1-2 mL of 1% lignocaine can be infused at the injection site to start with. Adverse effects are rare: oedema can occur, particularly with rapid infusion, but in one series of 1,850 infusions in 270 patients there were only four cases of local oedema and one of bruising[10].

Continuous subcutaneous infusion of drugs can be used as an alternative to intravenous or oral therapy for the administration of insulin or of opiates and antiemetics in palliative care, using a syringe-pump driver and small volumes of fluid (for example, 8 mL in 24 hours). However, care should be taken when using combinations of drugs in this way, because of potential pharmaceutical incompatibilities[11]. For example, immediate precipitation occurs when diamorphine hydrochloride 50 mg/mL and haloperidol 5 mg/mL are mixed; a lower concentration of haloperidol (0.75 mg/mL) must be used. Mixtures of diamorphine hydrochloride and cyclizine can also precipitate at high concentrations[12] and expert pharmaceutical advice should be sought.

Subcutaneous implantation

Subcutaneous injection or implantation of drugs such as goserelin, testosterone, and oestradiol is used to produce a prolonged effect, because absorption is slow. For example, although goserelin has a systemic elimination half-life of four hours, it can be given subcutaneously at intervals of one to three months during long-term treatment.

Conclusions

- Subcutaneous administration is easily performed and avoids many of the difficulties of the intravenous and intramuscular routes.
- Single subcutaneous injections also have the advantage of a slower rate of drug absorption than the intramuscular or intravenous routes.
- Continuous subcutaneous infusion is especially useful in palliative care for the administration of analgesic and antiemetic drugs and for hydration.
- Common adverse effects include pain at the site of injection, bruising and oedema.

References

1. Aronson JK. Routes of drug administration: 5. Intramuscular injection. *Prescribers' J* 1995; **35:** 32-6.
2. Besarab A. Optimizing epoetin therapy in end-stage renal disease: the case for subcutaneous administration. *Am J Kidney Dis* 1993; **22 (Suppl 1):** 13-22.
3. Erstad BL, Meeks ML. Influence of injection site and route on medication absorption. *Hosp Pharm* 1993; **28:** 953-78.
4. Pergallo-Dittko V. Aspiration of the subcutaneous insulin injection: clinical evaluation of needle size and amount of subcutaneous fat. *Diabetes Educ* 1995; **21:** 291-6.
5. Dann TC. Routine skin preparation before injection: an unnecessary procedure. *Lancet* 1969; **2:** 96-8.
6. Parham SM, Pasieka JL. Effect of pH modification by bicarbonate on pain after subcutaneous lidocaine injection. *Can J Surg* 1996; **39:** 31-5.
7. Mar AW, Dixon B, Ibrahim K, Parkin JD. Skin necrosis following subcutaneous heparin injection. *Australas J Dermatol* 1995; **36:** 201-3.
8. Schernthaner G. Immunogenicity and allergenic potential of animal and human insulins. *Diabetes Care* 1993; **16 (Suppl 3):** 155-65.

9.   Farrand S, Campbell AJ. Safe, simple subcutaneous fluid administration. *Br J Hosp Med* 1996; **55:** 690-2.
10. Schen RJ, Singer-Edelstein M. Subcutaneous infusions in the elderly. *J Am Geriatr Soc* 1981; **29:** 583-5.
11. Bradley K. Swap data on drug compatibilities. *Pharm Pract* 1996; **6:** 69-72.
12. Regnard C, Pashley S, Westrope F. Anti-emetic/diamorphine mixture compatibility in infusion pumps. *Br J Pharm Pract* 1986; **August:** 218-20.

Correspondence

reatment of anaphylactic reactions (Volume 37 Number 3, p125)

To the Editor:
We read Dr Ewan's article with interest, particularly regarding the route of adrenaline (epinephrine) administration.

We believe that a severe anaphylactic reaction occurring during anaesthesia should always be treated intravenously, not intramuscularly, the intravenous route and cardiac monitoring being available during general anaesthesia. The absorption of intramuscular adrenaline is reduced in profound hypotension or cardiovascular collapse, which are more likely to be caused by systemic allergens (such as drugs given intravenously during anaesthesia) than by food-induced reactions. Intramuscular adrenaline is suitable in food-induced reactions because these are commonly associated with respiratory difficulty and not hypotension.

Although intravenous adrenaline may increase the risk of myocardial infarction, ischaemia and arrhythmias, uncorrected profound hypotension due to unabsorbed intramuscular adrenaline will also have serious or fatal myocardial effects.

Department of Anaesthesia
Eastbourne District General Hospital
Kings Drive
East Sussex BN21 2UD

Anil Patel
Manesh Raval
Harry Walmsley
Nick Watson

Author's response:
Anaesthesia is a special situation. My article was aimed at anaphylaxis in general, but the advice on treatment also applies to anaphylaxis during anaesthesia although here there may be caveats. Guidelines for the management of adverse reactions during anaesthesia published by the Association of Anaesthetists and British Society for Allergy and Clinical Immunology[1] recommend intramuscular adrenaline, but include the option of intravenous administration.

Anaphylaxis induced by a drug given intravenously - such as an anaesthetic induction agent - is likely to be severe, with hypotension or cardiac collapse as the main feature. In food-induced anaphylaxis, hypotension is uncommon with airway obstruction the main danger. My article advises avoidance of intravenous adrenaline except in particular circumstances including severe circulatory collapse and during anaesthesia.

Intravenous administration of adrenaline is hazardous as it has to be titrated in slowly, using 1 in 10,000 strength, with cardiac monitoring. The anaesthetist is well placed to do this, having intravenous access and cardiac monitoring in place; it is inappropriate for a general practitioner or usually for the first responder in an accident and emergency (A&E) department. Early treatment of anaphylaxis is important and, in most circumstances, the most rapid way of giving adrenaline is by immediate intramuscular injection which frees one up to continue with other aspects of management.

Dr Patel and colleagues are concerned about absorption of adrenaline but my experience of treating anaphylaxis induced by desensitisation shows the intramuscular route to be rapidly effective, suggesting that there is no problem with absorption even in the face of hypotension.

There has been a vogue recently for paramedics and junior A&E staff to give intravenous adrenaline inappropriately, necessitating the production of new guidelines for paramedics[2]. This is potentially dangerous[3] and should be reserved for the particular circumstances described in my article. The key message is that adrenaline should be given intramuscularly.

Allergy and Clinical Immunology Clinic   **Pamela W Ewan**
Addenbrooke's Hospital
Cambridge CB2 2QQ

References
1. Association of Anaesthetists of Great Britain and Ireland, British Society of Allergy and Clinical Immunology. *Suspected anaphylactic reactions associated with anaesthesia.* 2nd rev. ed. London: The Association of Anaesthetists of Great Britain and Ireland, 1995.
2. Joint Royal Colleges and Ambulance Liaison Committee. Statement from the Resuscitation Council (UK) and the Joint Royal Colleges and Ambulance Liaison Committee. The use of adrenaline for anaphylactic shock (for ambulance paramedics). *J Joint Roy Coll Ambulance Liaison Committee* 1996; **1:** 1.
3. Sullivan TD. Cardiac disorders in penicillin-induced anaphylaxis: association with intravenous epinephrine therapy. *JAMA* 1982; **248:** 2161-2.

To the Editor:
Dr Ewan's excellent article omits two very important clinical features. She states that, while the time for a full-blown reaction varies, it is usually 10-30 minutes. It should be pointed out that the reaction can be biphasic and also that the time of onset of the first severe symptoms can be one hour or more. For example, in an analysis of 1,000 anaphylactic reactions to peanuts, 2.5% of patients reacted after one hour. This small group seems particularly at risk as in four out of seven of the deaths from anaphylaxis the symptoms began one hour or more after eating peanuts[1].

What is particularly important in any anaphylactic reaction is to find out whether the patient has asthma, as these patients are especially at risk of dying[1,2,3].

139 Harley Street   **A W Frankland**
London W1N 1DJ

References:
1. Frankland AW. Peanut allergy. *Cur Med Literature Allergy* 1996; **4:** 35-42.
2. Yunginger JW, Sweeney KG, Sturner WQ, et al. Fatal food-induced anaphylaxis. *JAMA* 1988; **260:** 1450-2.
3. Sampson HA, Mendelson L, Rosen JP. Fatal and near-fatal anaphylactic reactions to food in children and adolescents. *N Engl J Med* 1992; **327:** 380-4.

Author's response:
Dr Frankland makes two valuable points and I am grateful for his comments. It is important to recognise that biphasic and late-onset reactions may occur but that they must be rare. In extensive experience we have rarely seen the former, which may in part be influenced by my practice of giving hydrocortisone after adrenaline, but the majority of patients we see have been treated elsewhere. In a series of 500 peanut and tree-nut allergic patients, late onset reactions were seen in 0.4% (unpublished). In our experience of systemic allergic reactions of any cause, severe reactions are usually of early onset whereas late onset reactions tend to be less severe.

Allergy and Clinical Immunology Clinic   **Pamela W Ewan**
Addenbrooke's Hospital
Cambridge CB2 2QQ

Generic prescribing (Volume 37 Number 3, p133)

To the Editor:
Dr Mucklow does not mention an area of generic prescribing where the prescriber should be circumspect: that of prescribing for the elderly in whom multi-system pathology may dictate polypharmacy. As generically re-prescribing brand-name drugs which have been successfully used for many years can lead to confusion, anxiety and a loss of patient confidence in both drugs and doctor, such patients are

better left as they are. If changes must be made time should be set aside for advice, explanation and monitoring.

Specialist Registrar in General Medicine and Geriatrics   **Daryl Leung**
New Cross Hospital
Wolverhampton WV10 0QP

Author's response:
I agree that elderly patients are more vulnerable than the young to changes in the appearance of their medicines. In my article, I stated that "patients will generally consent to take a generic product...if one first explains the reasons behind the substitution, and reassures them about quality assurance and therapeutic equivalence". By implication, there will be some patients, of any age, who will not consent and in those circumstances no change need be made. The emphasis of the article lies in urging prescribers to communicate better and to prepare the ground carefully in collaboration with the community pharmacist, to minimise problems.   I do not believe that prescribers should be unduly circumspect about using generic products for the elderly, many of whom are perfectly able to understand the reasons for such substitution and more than ready to accept the change if they are warned.

Department of Medicines Management   **John C Mucklow**
Keele University
Keele ST5 5BG

Management of bronchiectasis (Volume 37 Number 3, p 151)

To the Editor:
As patients with bronchiectasis are at increased risk of pneumococcal infection, I would like to add to the annual influenza immunisation mentioned by Dr Wilson the importance of pneumococcal vaccination,

which is in keeping with Department of Health guidelines[1] for patients with chronic lung disease. Although most of these patients only require vaccination once in a lifetime, rates in susceptible individuals remain poor[2] - a considerable cause for concern in view of emerging antibiotic resistance in *Streptococcus pneumoniae*[3]. Concerted efforts are required to improve vaccination coverage for those at high risk and thereby minimise the significant morbidity and mortality associated with pneumococcal infection.

Clinical Research Fellow   **Aziz Sheikh**
Department of General Practice and Primary Health Care
Imperial College School of Medicine at St Mary's
London W2 1PG

References:
1. Department of Health, Welsh Office, Scottish Office Department of Health, Northern Ireland Department of Health and Social Services. *Immunisation against infectious disease 1996.* London: HMSO, 1996: 169-72.
2. McDonald P, Friedman EHI, Bank A, et al. Pneumococcal vaccine campaign based in general practice. *BMJ* 1997; **314:** 1094-8.
3. Speller DCE, Johnson AP, Cookson BD, Waight P, et al. PHLS surveillance of antibiotic resistance, England and Wales: emerging resistance in *Streptococcus pneumoniae. Emerg Infect Dis* 1996; **2:** 57-8.

Author's response:
Dr Sheikh makes an important point which is well taken. *Streptococcus pneumoniae* is less frequently a pathogen in bronchiectasis compared to chronic bronchitis and obstructive airways disease but, as patients with bronchiectasis do fall under the Department of Health guidelines for vaccinating patients with chronic lung disease, they should receive pneumococcal vaccination. The amount of protection this affords and the length of time it lasts are the subject of debate.

Royal Brompton Hospital   **Robert Wilson**
London SW3 6NP

Practical prescribing: Warfarin (Volume 37 Number 3, p173)

To the Editor:

I would like to comment on Professor Routledge's advice upon warfarin induction regimens, the one he suggests only being suitable for inpatient warfarinisation of previously heparinised patients.

Haematologists are seeing increasing numbers of patients referred to anticoagulant clinics with atrial fibrillation, when warfarin induction must be undertaken as an outpatient. In this setting it is safest to start the patient on 1 or 2 mg of warfarin and to escalate the dose at weekly or biweekly reviews until a therapeutic International Normalised Ratio (INR) is obtained. This avoids over-anticoagulating the patient, a danger in this group who may be taking a variety of drugs interacting with warfarin (including amiodarone and aspirin). It may also reduce the theoretical 'pro-thrombotic period' due to the relative depletion of proteins C and S that occurs early on in warfarinisation.

Specialist Registrar in Haematology   **A W Whiteway**
St Mary's Hospital
Praed Street
London W2 1NY

To the Editor:

In his review of warfarin, Professor Routledge does not mention prothrombotic states induced during the initiation of warfarin therapy. These may occur because the levels of some antithrombotic vitamin K-dependent factors, such as protein C, can fall faster than those of clotting factors II, VII, IX and X. This may explain warfarin-induced skin necrosis, a rare but potentially devasating complication which is commoner in people with protein C deficiency and, perhaps, other pro-thrombotic clotting factor abnormalities[1].

Theoretically, such complications may be less common in patients treated with heparin (which has been used in the treatment of warfarin-induced skin necrosis, and to allow warfarin therapy to be reintroduced in those previously suffering that complication[2]). In many situations, for example deep vein thrombosis, patients starting warfarin may already be receiving heparin but in others, for example atrial fibrillation, they may not. Could Professor Routledge offer any guidance on when heparin should be prescribed in this situation?

27 Sumner Place   **Andrew Weir**
London SW7 3NT

References
1. Roujeau, Stern RS. Severe adverse cutaneous reactions to drugs. *New Engl J Med* 1994; **331:** 1272-85.
2. Locht T, Lindstrom D. Severe skin necrosis following warfarin therapy in a patient with protein C deficiency. *J Intern Med* 1993; **233:** 287-9.

Author's response:

Dr Whiteway and Dr Weir both make the important point that loading doses of warfarin may need to be reduced and heparin cover given to patients with protein C or S deficiency. However, these are rare conditions in the general population and, unless there is a personal or family history of unexplained or recurrent thrombosis, it is most unlikely to be a problem. In the latter group, the possibility of protein C and S deficiency or other thrombophilic conditions should be considered and, if necessary, specialist advice sought.

The schedule Dr Whiteway describes for outpatients is likely to be safe, but if the dose is escalated by only 1 mg over two weeks, it may take over two months to anticoagulate even half the population (the mean dose requirement being around 5 mg per day). The schedule I described in the article has been used in outpatients without problem for many years and I am not aware of any cases of skin necrosis occurring during initiation with this flexible induction scheme, even in the absence of heparin cover. It is also unusual to obtain an INR above 4 with this schedule, and I have also used it in patients who are already on interacting drugs - eg, amiodarone. It does, of course, require measurement of daily INRs during the first four days.

University of Wales College of Medicine   **Philip A Routledge**
Cardiff CF4 4XN